P9-DID-747

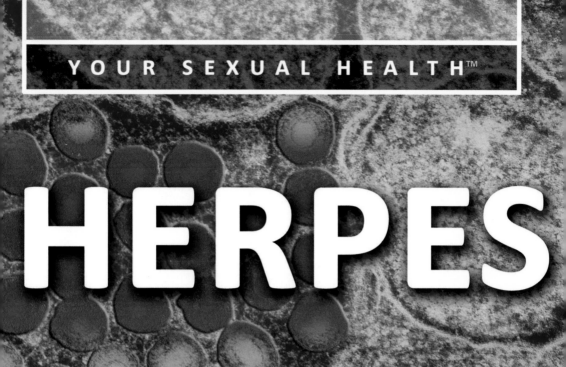

YOUR SEXUAL HEALTH™

HERPES

JERI FREEDMAN

ROSEN
PUBLISHING®

New York

Published in 2016 by The Rosen Publishing Group, Inc.
29 East 21st Street, New York, NY 10010

Copyright © 2016 by The Rosen Publishing Group, Inc.

First Edition

Library of Congress Cataloging-in-Publication Data

Freedman, Jeri.
Herpes/Jeri Freedman.
    pages cm.—(Your sexual health)
Includes bibliographical references and index.
Audience: Grades 7–12
ISBN 978-1-4994-6054-4 (library bound) — ISBN 978-1-4994-6055-1 (pbk.) —
ISBN 978-1-4994-6056-8 (6-pack)
1. Herpes genitalis—Popular works. I. Title.
RC203.H45F74 2016
616.9'112—dc23

                                                          2014040748

For many of the images in this book, the people photographed are models. The depictions do not imply actual situations or events

Manufactured in the United States of America

CONTENTS

Everywhere one looks, young people seem to be having sex—on television series, in the movies, in advertisements. Images of sex in the media get hormone-laden young adults to pay money for products being advertised, to download videos supported by advertisers, and to buy tickets to movies. On screens big and small, sex is shown as glamorous, daring, and romantic. Reality TV shows featuring rich, young people, in particular, give a distorted view of how the younger generation lives. Throughout the media, beautiful people fall into bed with no concern for the consequences. Rarely are the potential negative effects discussed.

The fact that sex permeates modern culture makes it seem as if everyone is doing it, and you're abnormal if you're not. The truth is very different. Don't believe everything your friends or schoolmates claim they've done. People

Popular culture emphasizes the sexual nature of teen relationships, but there are many ways to enjoy each other's company besides having sex.

like to sound as if they're popular and experienced. Many people exaggerate their sexual experience to impress their friends. Don't agree to have sex because you think "everyone else is." In reality, the trend among teenagers is to wait longer before having sex because of the dangers of sexually transmitted diseases (STDs).

Contrary to the image of teenagers portrayed in movies and popular TV shows, everyone is not constantly sleeping with everyone else. According to the Guttmacher Institute, 52 percent of seventeen-year-olds and nearly 40 percent of eighteen-year-olds have never had sex. In addition, casual sex is nowhere as common among young people as depicted in the media. Seventy percent of girls and 58 percent of boys stated that their first sexual experience was with a steady partner. According to a survey of high school students conducted by the U.S. Centers for Disease Control (CDC), two-thirds of students had not had sex in the three months prior to the study.

Despite peer pressure and the popularization of sex by the media, it is important to approach sex thoughtfully. In fact, having sex can have serious consequences for one's health. The danger of catching an STD should always be kept in mind. According to the CDC, "Nearly half of the 19 million new STDs each year are among young people aged 15–24 years." This statistic is not surprising given that the CDC reported that 40 percent of the students surveyed had not used a condom during their last sexual encounter.

Herpes is an especially problematic disease. Some STDs can be cured with medications such as penicillin. Herpes, however, cannot be cured. It has lifelong effects on one's health and social life.

The Herpes-Coldsores Support Network reported the following statistics on its website:

- Infection is more common in women (25 percent) than men (20 percent) because the virus is more easily passed from a man to a woman than the reverse.
- Approximately 25 percent of American adults have genital herpes.
- Approximately 46 percent of African Americans and 18 percent of Caucasians are infected in the United States.
- Approximately 20 percent of people in the United States over age twelve are infected with the HSV-2 strain of the herpes virus, which causes genital herpes.
- The number of people in the United States with herpes has increased 30 percent since the late 1970s, and the largest increase has been among white teenagers.
- Genital herpes is five times more common among twelve- to nineteen-year-old white teenagers and twice as common among twenty- to twenty-nine-year-olds.

These figures should make clear why it is important for you to learn more about herpes and to take precautions when engaging in sex.

CHAPTER ONE

The Herpes Virus

Herpes is a sexually transmitted disease. A sexually transmitted disease is an illness passed from one person to another during sexual activity. Some people think that STDs can be transmitted only via intercourse. In reality, STDs can also be transmitted during any type of

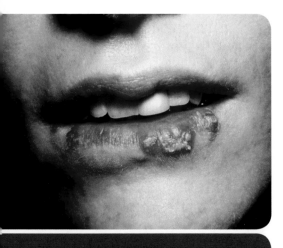

Herpes can affect various parts of the body. Oral sex can result in herpes sores such as these on the lips.

sex and are often caught during oral or anal sex. Sexually transmitted diseases are also called sexually transmitted infections (STIs) and venereal diseases (VDs). The types of organisms that transmit STDs include bacteria, parasites, and viruses. Herpes is a type of STD caused by a virus.

WHAT IS A VIRUS?

A virus is a microscopic particle that consists of a core of DNA (deoxyribonucleic acid) surrounded by a protective shell. The shell of the virus contains projections that allow it to attach to a cell and inject its DNA into it. The DNA contains the genetic blueprint for making more virus particles.

There are different types of herpes viruses. The herpes zoster virus causes chicken pox and shingles. The type of herpes virus that causes herpes is called the herpes simplex virus (HSV). There are two strains of HSV: HSV-1 and HSV-2. The HSV-1 strain can cause cold sores on the face or genital herpes. The HSV-2 strain causes herpes on the genitals, buttocks, anus, and thighs.

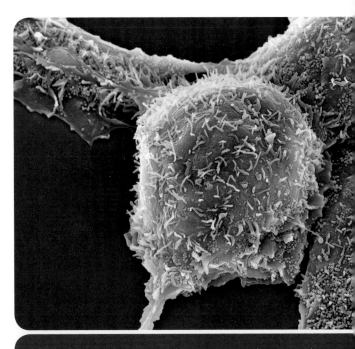

This scanning electron microscope photograph shows a cell infected with small, round herpes simplex 1 virus particles. These particles cause cold sores and genital herpes.

HOW A VIRUS INFECTS PEOPLE

To reproduce copies of itself, a virus must take over a cell in a living organism. Cells in the body consist of a central area, called the nucleus, surrounded by a membrane. Viruses like herpes infect people by attaching to the cell membrane and passing into the cell's nucleus, which contains the chromosomes that carry the cell's DNA. The cell has the ability to copy these chromosomes to make more cells like itself. When the virus invades a cell, it injects its DNA into the cell's nucleus. The virus uses the cell's own mechanisms to make copies of the viral DNA instead of the cell's and to encase the new DNA in copies of its own outer coating. When the cell is filled with copies of the virus, it bursts open. The virus spreads to nearby cells, and the process is repeated.

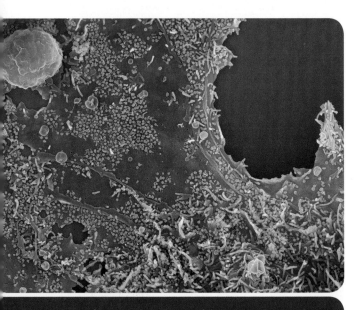

Herpes virus particles (green) are seen being released from a host cell. This virus infects cells around the mouth. Once a person is infected, the virus remains in his or her body for life.

HOW TO AVOID HERPES

The following are some tips for avoiding genital herpes:

- Have sex with only one partner. This may mean waiting to have sex until you are in a long-term relationship or married. The more people you have sex with, the greater your chances of catching genital herpes.
- If you do have sex, use a latex condom. This will reduce the chances of catching the disease.
- If you have sex with someone who has herpes, avoid sex during active outbreaks when symptoms are present, and have your partner take an antiviral medication to inhibit the virus.
- Wash after having sex or having any contact with herpes sores. The outer coating of the virus is composed of a type of fat called a lipid. Soap appears to destroy this lipid coating and also washes the virus particles off the skin's surface.
- Avoid behavior that may cloud your judgment, such as drinking and taking recreational drugs. These kinds of conduct can lead you to engage in risky behavior, including unsafe sex.

HOW IS HERPES SPREAD?

Herpes is a viral infection of the skin. Herpes is transferred from one person to another by skin-to-skin contact. The virus particles on one person's skin move into the second person's body through any opening in the skin or mucous membranes (such as those in the mouth or vaginal lining). Once the virus particles are in a person's body, they can infect that person's cells and be passed on to other people. The herpes virus most commonly affects the genitals or mouth, although it can also infect other areas such as the buttocks, thighs, or eyes. On the mouth it produces cold sores; on the fingers, the infection is called whitlows. Occasionally, herpes affects other areas of the skin. The herpes virus is passed only by skin-to-skin contact, not through blood. Therefore, it is not transferable via contact with an infected person's blood or through a blood transfusion. People are most likely to be infectious when they are experiencing active symptoms of herpes. However, the virus can sometimes be transferred from the skin when a person is not having symptoms.

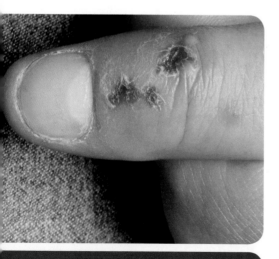

The herpes virus can infect the skin on any part of the body, including the hands. Because it is passed by skin-to-skin contact, washing after contact is very important.

MYTHS AND FACTS

MYTH
Only people who have many sexual partners are likely to get herpes.

FACT
Herpes is very common, and anyone can catch it during sex.

MYTH
Herpes is spread by contact with blood.

FACT
Herpes is transferred by skin-to-skin contact and is not present in the blood.

MYTH
A person knows if he or she has herpes.

FACT
Many people who have herpes don't know they have it because they have no symptoms or mild symptoms.

CHAPTER TWO

Herpes:
The Creeping Disease

The transmission of diseases by organisms such as viruses was not understood until modern times. However, herpes infections have been observed and studied since ancient times.

HISTORY OF HERPES

Herpes infections were common as far back as ancient Greece. The Greek physician Hippocrates (c. 460–c. 370 BCE) described how herpes was spread by contact with infected skin. Ancient Greek scholars dubbed the disease "herpes," from the Greek word *herpein*, meaning to creep or crawl. They gave it this name because of the way the herpes sores spread across skin.

In 1736, French king Louis XIV's physician, John Astuc, reported that herpes was linked with genital contact. The first book on genital herpes

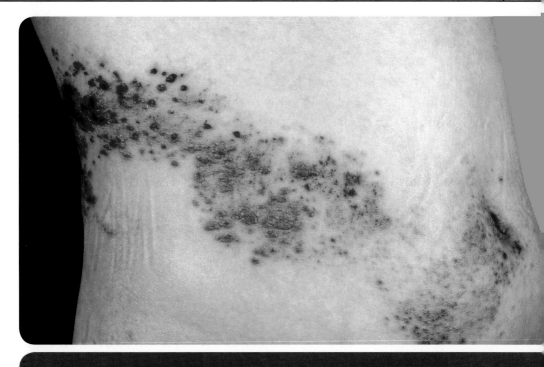

The rash caused by the herpes virus spreads across the skin; therefore, the ancient Greeks named it the creeping disease.

was *Les Herpes Genitaux*, published in 1886 by two French doctors, Charles-Paul Diday and Adrien Doyon. They recommended a number of herpes treatments, including using bismuth and starch poultices (a hot mass of bread or meal and herbs placed on the skin). They also suggested that people with herpes refrain from using alcohol and tobacco and avoid sexual excess. (This latter is still good advice today.)

In the early twentieth century, studies of cells infected with herpes showed that giant cells with multiple nuclei were associated with the herpes virus infection. In 1919, a scientist named A. Lowenstein was able to confirm by experiment that HSV was infectious. In 1925, an American virologist, Ernest Goodpasture, proved that herpes viruses infect the central nervous system as well as the skin, traveling through nerves rather than the bloodstream. The theory of latency was developed by Australian microbiologist Frank MacFarlane Burnet in 1939. According to this theory, the herpes virus, when attacked by the immune system, becomes dormant in the roots of nerves. Later the virus can become reactivated, causing another outbreak of herpes symptoms. In this way, the herpes virus differs from many other infectious organisms, which are destroyed by the immune system. Herpes sufferers can experience recurring outbreaks of the disease throughout their lives. Burnet lacked the scientific tools to prove his theory. However, it was confirmed by scientists Jack Stevens and Marjorie Cook in 1971.

Methods of treating herpes began to be developed in the 1960s. These treatments were based on inhibiting the viral DNA so the virus could not replicate (make copies of) itself. Herpes was first officially designated a sexually transmitted disease in 1970. In 1978, Gertrude B. Elion developed the first antiviral prescription medication for herpes. Antiviral prescription medications became available for general use in the 1980s.

Dr. Gertrude B. Elion is a Nobel Prize–winning biochemist who developed many important medications, including acyclovir (Zovirax), for viral herpes.

HOW HERPES AFFECTS THE BODY

Herpes can produce a wide range of symptoms. It can produce blisters or sores. In other cases, it just causes a rash. There is a lot of misinformation about the effects of herpes. Typically, the visual symptoms are blisterlike sores. These sores start as blisters, open up, and then develop a scab. Those infected with herpes may also experience itching, swollen glands, fever, headache, muscle aches, and burning while passing urine.

There are several factors that determine how virulent the herpes virus is. Among these are a gene called *ICP47* and one called *ICP34.5.* These genes interfere with the functioning of elements of the immune system that would otherwise attack the virus.

Some people think that herpes causes cervical cancer. This notion is false. Cervical cancer is caused by a different virus, the human papilloma virus (HPV). However, taking precautions to protect yourself from catching herpes can also help protect you from other viruses, such as HPV.

HOW THE BODY REACTS TO HERPES

The body controls HSV infection through the actions of the immune system. The immune system produces cells that fight viruses and other foreign organisms that invade the body. Some of these cells are produced in bone marrow in the arm and leg bones, and some are produced in the lymph nodes, small glands located throughout the body. The cells produced by the immune system travel through the blood vessels and through lymphatic vessels, which are similar to blood vessels but are filled with a fluid called lymph rather than blood.

Two major types of cells that fight the HSV virus are natural killer (NK) cells and T cells. (The "T" represents "thymus," which is the organ in which these cells usually mature.) NK

HOW TO ASK A PARTNER ABOUT STDS

People take unnecessary risks because they are embarrassed to ask whether a boyfriend or girlfriend has an STD. Even if you aren't having sex now, this is an important skill to learn for the future. Remember, STDs are medical conditions, and it's up to you to protect your health. If you're embarrassed, say so. Tell the person you're seeing that it's awkward to talk about the subject, but everyone knows that you both have to protect your health. Prepare the key points of what you want to say before having the discussion. It's much easier to speak about a difficult topic if you have worked out what you want to say in advance. Explain that you're not suggesting that your partner has an STD, but before you have sex, you should talk about your past history because often people have an STD without even knowing about it.

Insist that if you have sex, you should use a condom. If your partner agrees and has had sex before, suggest that you should both get tested for STDs so you can start your new sexual relationship with confidence. It doesn't hurt to have noted a clinic or two where you can be tested and the cost. Sometimes reluctance turns out to be more financial than personal.

If the other person refuses to discuss STDs or drops you because you asked about them, this is a sign that something is wrong with either the person or the relationship.

cells are able to identify the infection in cells. When an NK cell finds an affected cell, it kills the cell, keeping the virus from using it to replicate any more viruses. T cells target the virus particles themselves. The T cells produce antibodies, which are Y-shaped proteins. The antibodies attach, or bind, to the virus, making it impossible for it to engage in any further activity. The first time a person is infected with a virus like herpes, the immune system has to produce antibodies to that particular virus from scratch. Once the body has created antibodies to that virus, they continue to circulate in the body to protect it in the future. That is why the first outbreak of herpes is usually the worst. Subsequent outbreaks are usually shorter and less severe, because the existing antibodies can deactivate the virus more quickly.

Because there is no cure for

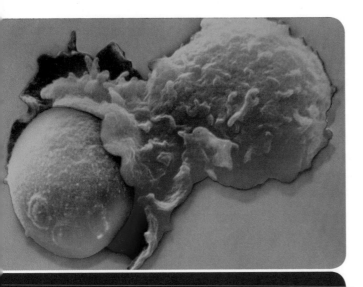

This scanning electron microscope photograph shows an immune system cell called a lymphocyte engulfing a particle that could infect a cell in the body.

herpes, the role of the immune system in controlling the herpes virus is especially important. Therefore, keeping the immune system healthy is critical. In most cases, herpes doesn't affect organs other than the skin. However, in those with a weakened immune system, it can affect other parts of the body, including the brain, esophagus, lungs, eyes, liver, and spinal cord. Among those with weakened immune systems are:

- Individuals who have acquired immunodeficiency syndrome (AIDS) or have been infected with the HIV virus, which causes AIDS.
- People who are on medications to suppress the immune system, as a treatment for diseases related to the immune system, such as lupus or Crohn's disease.
- Individuals who take medications to suppress the immune system because of an organ transplant.
- Those who are under stress for long periods of time. Stress causes the body to secrete chemicals called corticosteroids, which help the body function under stress. These chemicals have the side effect of suppressing the immune system.
- People who are very young or very old. In the former, the immune system has yet to fully develop, and in the latter it functions less well.

If you do contract herpes, it is important to make sure any doctor you see knows about it, especially before you undergo any treatment that involves suppressing the immune system.

RECURRENCES

Not everyone who has an episode of herpes experiences further outbreaks. Those who do often find that subsequent outbreaks are less severe than the first episode because the immune system already has antibodies to the virus and can respond more quickly and effectively. Subsequent outbreaks of herpes are preceded by symptoms such as tingling, itching, burning, or pain, which serve as a warning that an outbreak is about to occur. People experiencing these warning signs may want to start taking an antiviral medication to reduce the symptoms of an outbreak.

Recurrence of herpes is most likely in those infected with HSV-2. According to the CDC, about 80 percent of people with HSV-2 have at least one recurrence, whereas only 50 percent of those infected with HSV-1 do. Also, those infected with HSV-2 are likely to have an outbreak several times each year, whereas HSV-1 outbreaks usually occur much less frequently, usually only once per year. The occurrence of outbreaks varies from person to person, however. Outbreaks are most likely in the first year or two after infection and tend to decrease over time.

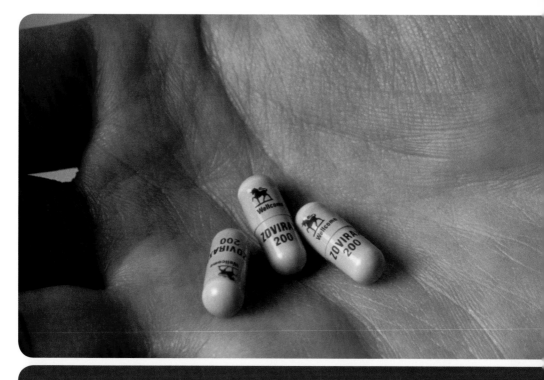

These capsules contain the antiviral medication acyclovir, with the brand named Zovirax, which is primarily used to treat herpes.

Although it is not known exactly why the virus reactivates at various times, the factors that influence outbreaks are known. Common factors include being run down, having one's period, prolonged exposure of the affected area to sunlight, catching another STD, drinking large amounts of alcohol, being under stress for an extended period, and depression. Note that many of these factors make an outbreak more likely because they negatively affect the activity of the immune system, which normally keeps the virus in check.

HOW HERPES IS TRANSMITTED

Herpes is transmitted when the virus is shed from the skin of an infected person. Shedding occurs when the herpes virus becomes active and travels down nerve fibers to the surface of the skin. When herpes is present on the skin or in an active sore, this is called viral shedding. Viral shedding can take place with or without active symptoms. However, it is more common when symptoms are present. The virus being shed can pass into the body of another person through any opening in the skin or mucous membrane.

TRANSMISSION TO A BABY

Because herpes is not transmitted through the blood, it is not passed from mother to child during pregnancy. Therefore, there is no reason for a person with herpes to avoid having children. However, if an infection is active at the time a woman gives birth, there is a chance she could pass the infection along to the child through skin-to-skin contact. Therefore, if you do contract herpes and become pregnant, it is important to inform your obstetrician so he or she can take appropriate precautions. In most cases, women with herpes can have normal vaginal delivery. However, in some cases, if a woman has an active genital infection at the time of delivery, the baby may be delivered by Caesarian section (an incision in the abdomen).

In most cases, parents with herpes can have normal contact with the infant. Because herpes is easily deactivated and removed by soap and water, simply maintaining normal cleanliness is sufficient. However, it's best to avoid kissing a baby during the first six months of life if active cold sores are present, because an infant's immune system is not fully developed and it may not be able to fight off infection. By six months, the child's immune system should be fully functional and capable of warding off the virus.

CHAPTER THREE

Don't Do It!

How you behave and the decisions you make in regard to having sex are the major factors in putting yourself at risk or protecting yourself from infection with herpes and other STDs. It is important to remember that when you put yourself at risk, you are also contributing to the potential spread of the disease and putting others at risk as well. This case is especially true of herpes, whose symptoms are not always apparent. Therefore, it is important to behave responsibly.

PUTTING YOURSELF AT RISK

The major factor in the spread of STDs is having unprotected sex. When you do have sex, be sure to use a condom. Be aware that only latex condoms protect against the spread of viruses such as herpes. Even using a condom does not guarantee 100 percent protection against catching herpes, so it is important to take other precautions. The more partners you have sex with, the more likely you are to be exposed to the

Condoms are readily available and should always be used when having sex. Using them can help significantly when trying to avoid catching diseases like herpes spread by skin-to-skin contact.

infection. Restricting your sexual relations to one person with whom you have a relationship is safer than having lots of casual sex.

The decision whether or not to have sex requires a clear mind and good judgment. Using recreational (party) drugs or drinking alcohol affects your judgment and also reduces your inhibitions. Inhibitions are the feelings that prevent you from doing something because it will have a negative effect. People who take drugs or get drunk often do things they suffer the effects of long after the drug or alcohol has worn off.

RESISTING PRESSURE

Do not allow yourself to be talked into having sex before you're ready. How will you know if you're ready? If you feel uncomfortable when the subject comes up, you are probably not ready. If you haven't given any thought to having sex with a person you've been dating, you shouldn't do so until you've thought the matter through. Tell the person you need to think about it. You shouldn't have sex to seem cool, to fit in, to be popular, or because people will think you're a nerd if you don't. Having sex for these reasons is unlikely to attract people, except those who want to use you. You should never agree to have sex with someone because you are embarrassed to say you don't want to. Just say you're not ready, need to think about it, or have decided to wait.

It's absolutely acceptable today to tell a person you like him or her but don't want to have sex yet. Many young people are choosing abstinence, some for religious reasons and some for health reasons. Some simply don't want to risk pregnancy before they prepare themselves for a career or find out what they really want in life. Don't be afraid to say no because the person who asks might reject you. If someone cares about you, he or she will care about more than having sex. If a person does drop you because you won't have sex, this can be upsetting—but

It's important to have a serious discussion with a potential partner before engaging in sex. There are both health and relationship issues that you need to discuss.

it also reveals that he or she was not in love with you. That person is not likely to be the only person you will be involved with for the rest of your life!

As an added precaution, you can use the buddy system. If you go to clubs and parties, take a friend and agree that you will stop each other from doing something you will later regret. Often a friend telling you to stop doing something foolish is all it takes to avoid trouble.

HOW TO SAY NO

A lot of young people of both genders don't know what to say when pressured to have sex. Teller County, Colorado, Public Health published on its website (www.co.teller.co.us/publichealth/101WaysToSayNoToSex.aspx) a list of responses used by real high school students to say no. The following are a few of these:

I've decided to wait.
How about a movie instead?
I'm not ready.
You're crazy.
I want to be loved, not make love.
I can't support a child.
Not until we're married.
If you loved me, you wouldn't ask.
School comes before sex.
It's against my religion/values.
We're too young.
I don't feel comfortable.
With all these diseases going around?
Not everybody's doing it. I'm not.
We can find other ways to express our love.
Have you thought about consequences?
Ask me again in five years.

Thanks anyway.
I don't want that kind of pressure.
No.
I said no, and I mean it!

Keep in mind that if everyone were doing it, the website wouldn't have 101 ways to say no from actual high school students.

MAINTAINING GOOD SEXUAL HEALTH

There are a number of skills that are useful for maintaining good sexual health and fostering good relationships. There are both physical and mental aspects to maintaining good sexual health. Among the mental aspects is developing good communication, goal-setting, and decision-making skills. These skills are useful for any important decision you make in life, including if and when to have sex and how to do so in a safe way.

Goal setting is the process of deciding what you want in various aspects of your life. Knowing this allows you to plan accordingly and focus on achieving those ends. Make a list of what you want in terms of personal relationships and other aspects of your life.

Examples of goal-setting questions are as follows:

- What kind of physical shape do I want to be in?
- What kind of career do I want?
- What kind of personal life do I want? Marriage? Family?
- What kind of lifestyle do I want to have in the future?

Once you have the answers to these questions, you can come up with steps to achieve these goals. This process will provide you with the motivation to behave in a manner that will maximize your chances of having what you want in the future. Remembering your goals will strengthen your resolve when dealing with people who want you to do things that are not in your best interest.

Decision-making skills are tools to help you make choices that are best for you. First, clearly state the decision to be made. Next, research information that can affect whether or not you should do the activity in question. List the pros and cons of each possible course of action, and choose the best option. To a large extent, your decisions as to what is best will be based on your goals.

Communication skills allow you to communicate clearly and comfortably with other people. They are especially important in situations that may be awkward, such as discussing sex. Preparation is one key to good communication. If you don't feel you're ready to have sex or don't feel comfortable asking a potential partner about exposure to diseases, spend some time thinking about what you'll say if you are asked to have sex, or role-play with a friend so that you're prepared when the subject comes up. Another aspect of communication is talking to others, friends or professionals, for advice. Often people feel they must decide things for themselves,

You might want to discuss how to stay healthy sexually with a medical professional, who might have valuable suggestions. He or she might be able to provide you with other resources as well.

but talking to others may provide ideas you haven't thought of. Other people may have dealt with similar situations and developed ways of responding that can be of use to you. They can also provide another perspective (or view) of the situation.

From a physical perspective, it is important to make sure you are healthy and to detect any problems as soon as possible. If you do become sexually active, have regular checkups by a physician. He or she will be able to observe any potential problems you may not be aware of. If you experience any discomfort in the area of your genitals or the lower area of your body, or if you have any unusual discharge, see your doctor immediately. If you have been sexually active and have not been tested for common sexually transmitted diseases, you should get these tests. If you have an issue, prompt treatment will increase your chances of addressing it and minimizing discomfort.

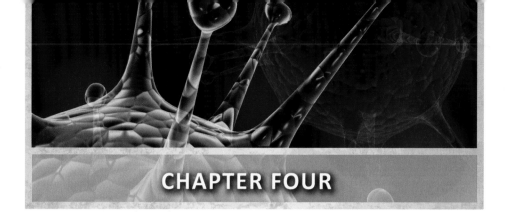

CHAPTER FOUR

Catching Herpes . . . What Now?

As with most diseases, the sooner you find out that you have herpes, the better. You should have regular checkups, and let your doctor know immediately if you have any symptoms.

HOW IS HERPES DIAGNOSED?

Doctors do not test for herpes routinely during an examination or when doing standard tests such as Pap smears on a woman. For herpes to be identified, a person must have symptoms. If a patient has sores that might be herpes, the doctor will take a swab of the area. This process consists of taking a sample of the fluid from the sores using a cotton swab, much like the ones used in TV cop shows for getting DNA samples. The swab is sent to a lab for testing, by means of a cell culture. They will put the material on the swab in a medium containing nutrients,

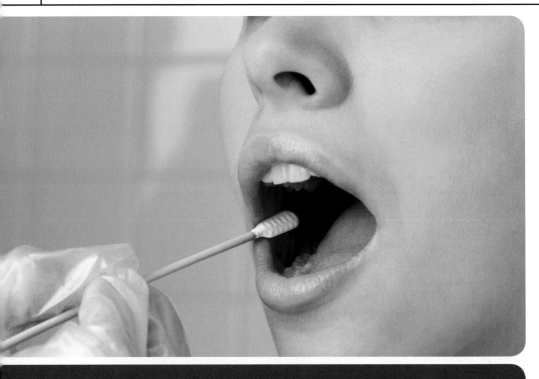

A swab is used to collect cells for examination. This process enables the cells to be examined directly under a powerful microscope to see if they contain virus particles.

and see if they can grow cells that show the virus when looked at under the microscope. There are some issues with the cell culture approach. It can produce a false negative (showing that you don't have the disease when you do) if the infection is very recent or the sores are nearly healed. It can also sometimes produce a false positive (showing that you are infected when you're not). Therefore, if your behavior is such that it's unlikely you've been infected, the test may need to be repeated.

Another test for the herpes virus is the polymerase chain reaction (PCR). In this test, a sample of the viral DNA is compared to the known profile of the DNA of the herpes virus. This test is extremely accurate, but it is more complicated to perform and therefore more expensive than a cell culture.

Immunofluorescence antibody tests can also be used to test for the presence of the herpes virus. This type of test relies on the fact that when foreign particles enter your body, your immune system produces antibodies, which bind to the particles and deactivate them. In an immunofluorescence test, a fluorescent dye is combined with a sample that may contain the herpes virus. Antibodies for HSV are added to the sample, and if the virus is present, the antibodies attach to it. The antibodies are

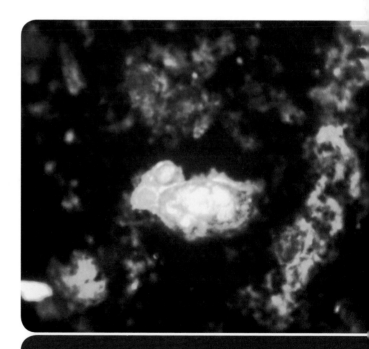

This photograph taken through a microscope shows a herpes virus particle glowing in an immunofluorescence test, making it easy to identify.

then separated from the rest of the sample and examined under a special light. If viruses are attached to the antibodies, they glow under the light. Because each type of antibody will attach only to a particular virus, the fluorescence shows that the herpes virus is present. Because there are different antibodies for HSV-1 and HSV-2, this test can identify which strain of herpes a person has.

Although these tests will identify the fact you have been exposed to herpes, they will not indicate when that occurred, only that the virus is in your system. Exposure could have occurred recently or a long time in the past.

FORMS OF TREATMENT

There is no cure for herpes. However, there are treatments that can reduce the effects of symptoms when an outbreak occurs. The medications used to treat herpes are called antiviral drugs because they fight viruses. These medications can reduce how long symptoms last and how severe they are. They can also help people with herpes stay symptom-free longer. Among the drugs commonly used to treat genital herpes symptoms are acyclovir (Zovirax), famciclovir (Famvir), and valacyclovir (Valtrex). Most commonly these drugs are taken as pills. Acyclovir is also sometimes given intravenously (through the vein) for severe

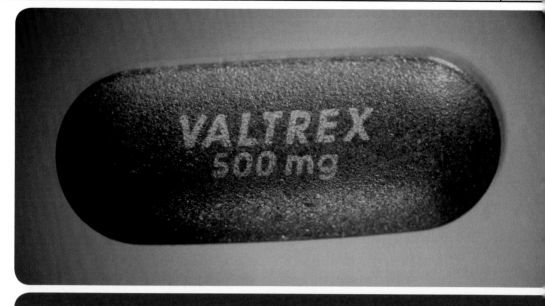

Valtrex (valacyclovir HCL) is a medication for herpes. It slows the spread of the herpes virus in the body, allowing the body's immune system to fight the virus.

cases. To be effective, antiviral medications must be taken internally. Applying medications to the skin has little effect.

Treatment is usually given when a person first has signs of an outbreak. Usually, an antiviral medication is given in pill form for seven to ten days. The goal is to improve symptoms or keep them from getting worse. If the sores have not healed at the end of that time, a second round of medication may be given. Some doctors give patients a prescription for an antiviral drug they can keep on hand to use whenever a flare-up starts. In cases where a person has frequent outbreaks, a doctor may prescribe an antiviral drug to take every day rather than only when a flare-up occurs. This approach suppresses the viruses and can significantly reduce or eliminate outbreaks. Suppressive therapy can also reduce the chances of passing on the virus. Nonetheless, those who have been infected should use a condom. Luckily, antiviral drugs usually have few side effects.

Be aware that there are many marketers promoting "cures" and "remedies" for chronic (long-term) diseases such as herpes, including special diets and creams. People promoting a "natural" cure sometimes recommend topical substances like coconut oil or petroleum jelly. There is no evidence that these compounds have any effect on the virus (although it's possible that some may have a slight mechanical effect by reducing friction from other tissue rubbing on sores). Also, in most cases, good old soap and water is just as effective as antibacterial solutions and gels for removing viruses and bacteria from your skin.

STAYING HEALTHY

Stress and poor health make herpes outbreaks more likely because of their negative effects on the immune system. Your immune system is your main line of defense against the herpes virus. Keeping your immune system in good shape will allow it to do the best job possible of fighting the virus. To do this, you need to eat a healthy, well-balanced diet. Eat lean protein, vegetables, and grains without too much fat and sugar. A healthy diet ensures that your body has the nutrients it needs.

It is also important to get enough sleep. Many young people today are sleep-deprived, staying up late when they need to get up early for school and other activities. Getting too little sleep affects your mental and physical health and can make your immune system work less effectively. Eating and sleeping right improve your body's strength and energy.

Eating a good diet is important to staying healthy and keeping your immune system working well. This practice is especially important if you have a disease such as herpes.

Don't smoke. Smoking damages many organs in the body, making your body less able to fight infection. Getting exercise can also help your body stay in good shape. Having herpes should not keep you from working out or participating in sports. The herpes virus is not spread through casual contact, so it is not going to affect other people in a locker room.

Avoid excessive use of alcohol and use of recreational drugs. These can affect the general health of your body and make it less able to fight off infections, including herpes. Using alcohol and recreational drugs can also impair your judgment, making it more likely that you will engage in negative behaviors, including unprotected sex.

Most common medications do not affect the immune system. However, some diseases, such as rheumatoid arthritis, lupus, psoriasis, and some forms of cancer, are at times treated with medications that suppress the immune system. Before starting any treatment or medication that might affect your immune system, tell the doctor that you have herpes. He or she may need to adjust your treatment or give you antiviral medication to prevent an outbreak of the disease.

To stay as healthy as possible and catch any issues as soon as possible, you should see your doctor regularly for checkups—at least once every year. This practice allows the doctor to notice any changes in your condition and treat them rapidly.

PROTECTING YOUR PARTNERS AND YOURSELF

It is important to understand that when you have herpes, you can spread it to other

TELLING A PARTNER YOU HAVE HERPES

People—with and without STDs—tend to become fixated on how they are going to deal with sex as soon as they think about dating someone. But you don't have to focus a potential relationship on sex. It's fine to go out with someone just to see if you like the same things and have feelings for each other, especially when you're young. If you do decide you're ready to have sex, then you need to talk to the other person about the fact that you have herpes. Don't wait until you are about to have sex—or worse, until after you've had it.

Be prepared to explain what herpes is and that there are steps to take to minimize infection. Yes, there's a chance the other person will reject you, but if he or she does so before knowing the facts about the disease, there's a good chance that he or she didn't really care for you anyway. If someone is nasty about it, you're well rid of him or her. Remember, if you date, you're likely to experience breakups from a number of causes along the way to finding the right person. If you keep looking, you'll find a person who listens when you explain about the disease and cares enough about you to deal with it. You may even find someone who has also been exposed to the disease, since it's relatively common. Remember, having herpes doesn't keep you from having a marriage and family, if that's what you want.

people but only by having sex. The chances of spreading herpes to someone else are greatest when you have an active outbreak. Therefore, it's best to avoid sex when you have active symptoms or sores, until all the sores are healed. Keep in mind that herpes is often spread via oral sex, so you should avoid this activity when you have active cold sores. Using a condom during oral sex as well as intercourse can provide protection. If you or your partner experiences frequent severe outbreaks, taking an antiviral medication on a regular basis may be appropriate.

Herpes is rarely spread from one person to another other than by having sex. Using the same toilet, towels, and the like will not spread the virus, as it cannot survive outside the body. In addition, it is easily removed by the use of soap and water. If you have an active infection and will be in contact with someone whose immune system may not be fully active, such as a baby or a very elderly person, you simply need to wash your hands first. Also, it is a good idea not to kiss anyone with a compromised immune system if you have cold sores. At other times, it should be OK to do so.

Above all, you should know you can live a perfectly normal life and, if you wish, have a family.

10 GREAT QUESTIONS
TO ASK A MEDICAL PROFESSIONAL

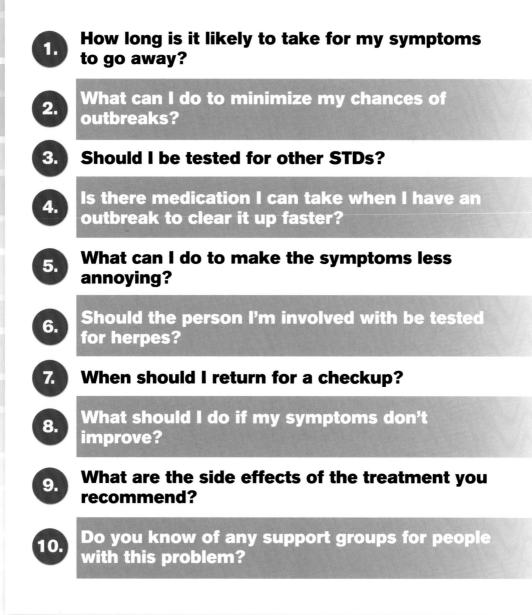

1. How long is it likely to take for my symptoms to go away?

2. What can I do to minimize my chances of outbreaks?

3. Should I be tested for other STDs?

4. Is there medication I can take when I have an outbreak to clear it up faster?

5. What can I do to make the symptoms less annoying?

6. Should the person I'm involved with be tested for herpes?

7. When should I return for a checkup?

8. What should I do if my symptoms don't improve?

9. What are the side effects of the treatment you recommend?

10. Do you know of any support groups for people with this problem?

CHAPTER FIVE

Coping with Herpes

Herpes can affect you emotionally as well as physically. First, there is the stress of having to deal with a chronic disease. If you are prone to recurrences, you will have to make sure you have appropriate medication, and you will have to take care not to subject yourself to undue stress or engage in behaviors that are likely to lead to flare-ups. Second, there is the awkwardness of needing to tell potential partners that you have herpes, which can be stressful. However, there are resources that can help you cope with having herpes.

THE EMOTIONAL EFFECTS OF HERPES

Finding out that you have herpes can result in feelings of sadness, anger, and confusion. You may feel angry at the person who passed the disease on to you and angry at yourself for letting it happen. You may experience rejection or feel stigmatized because you have an STD. A stigma is any characteristic that causes one to be devalued by other people.

You may also find yourself withdrawing from other people because you believe that they will reject you or think less of you. Cutting yourself off from other people can have negative effects, leaving you feeling alone and isolated. This can make your situation more traumatic at a time when you are unsure of how to deal with the disease. Feeling stigmatized can lead to self-consciousness and low self-esteem.

Finding out you have herpes can be stressful, but isolating yourself will make it more difficult to obtain the support and information you need.

Support is very important when dealing with a condition like herpes. There are a variety of resources to which you can turn for support and help.

TELLING YOUR PARENTS

Telling your parents you have an STD can be very stressful. Some people are reluctant to tell their parents because they are afraid they will be angry or disappointed. However, there are advantages to doing so. First, they are in the position to help you get appropriate medical care. Second, your family can be a source of emotional support. Be aware that parents love their children and want to help them. Even if they are upset to hear you have the disease, they will probably want to help you. Their help can provide both practical and emotional support when you are dealing with the problem. They are more likely than you

Talk to your parents if you find you're infected with herpes. You are important to them, and they will want to help you. They have valuable knowledge and experience.

to know about or be able to find appropriate medical resources. Indeed, they are likely to already have a gynecologist (for women) or urologist (for men) who can help you. They can also provide you with emotional support when dealing with the problem. You can literally cry on your mother's shoulder. Having someone else to help you deal with the problem can relieve the stress of dealing with it on your own. Also, trying to keep the condition a secret from your family will add to your stress, which is not good for you mentally or physically. And parents are very good at sensing when something is wrong with their child, so in the long run, keeping it a secret may not work. Although in many states it's legal for doctors to treat teenaged patients for sexual issues without telling their parents, your parents may get a bill or a summary of charges from their insurance company if you see your doctor. It's better for them to find out about the issue from you than from a letter in the mail. It shows trust and the fact that you are depending on them to help you.

That said, there are a few guidelines that are helpful. Make sure that you pick a time and place when you can discuss the matter at length without distractions. It's often a good idea to pick the parent you feel most comfortable with and talk to him or her first. That parent can help you tell the other one once you've talked about the situation and will make the discussion feel less like a confrontation. Admit you're nervous about talking to them; that will help make the situation feel less awkward. You may want to tell your parents you need their help with a problem. That will focus the discussion on the problem, rather than on the behavior that led to it. Parents are quick to spring to their children's aid when they are in trouble. So this approach may help turn the discussion into one of working together. When you tell your parents, they may not know what the implications of having herpes are. It's a good idea to gather some information about herpes before you tell them you have been exposed. That way, you can reassure them that it won't keep you from having a normal life or a family. It may be useful to suggest seeing a doctor together, so they have the facts regarding the disease. Depending on your age, you may find that what shocks them the most is the fact that you have been sexually active. However, that is a part of growing up. Remember that your parents were once teenagers, too, and all the choices they made weren't correct. No matter how upset they are about the situation, taking care of you is still likely to be their major concern.

If for some reason you feel you can't tell your parents, you still need to take care of your health. There are resources such as Planned Parenthood and community clinics where you can get tested for STDs and that can recommend resources for you.

STRESS REDUCTION AND HERPES

The more stressed out you are about having herpes, the more your body will put out chemicals that suppress your immune system, which makes outbreaks more likely. In turn, the more outbreaks you have, the more stressed you are likely to become. To break this cycle, it is useful to learn some stress-reduction techniques such as meditation, progressive muscle relaxation, or behavioral stress management (which teaches you how to control stress-producing behavior and thoughts). There are many books and workshops on these techniques. Your doctor, a local community mental health center, or one of the support organizations for herpes can recommend resources for stress management.

It is important to remember that you are not the disease. Do not allow yourself to be defined by the fact that you have herpes. Many people have chronic diseases and other issues such as handicaps they must cope with. Having herpes is merely one small aspect of your overall self and should not keep you from having a normal and fulfilling life.

RESOURCES FOR COPING WITH HERPES

Your first line of support is your friends and family. Talking to them about your feelings can help relieve some of the stress of having the disease. Do not feel you have to go it alone. You cannot pass herpes to other people except by having sex with them, so spend time with your friends. Not only can they provide emotional support, but they can also distract you so you aren't obsessing about the problem. The more you engage in normal social activities, the better you'll feel emotionally.

Hanging out with friends and having their support and engaging in activities with them can be a great stress reducer. Herpes is only one factor in your life.

The second line of support is a professional, such as a psychiatrist, psychologist, or counselor. These experts have the training to help individuals cope with trauma and stress. They are especially useful if having herpes leads you to experience depression (an excessive feeling of sadness). They are also an excellent source for learning coping techniques such as methods of relaxation.

A third source of help is support groups. These groups consist of people who all suffer from the same or similar disorders. In a support group, you do not have to fear a negative reaction to the fact that you have a disease. Because the people in the group have the same problem, they know how you feel. Those who have had the problem for a long time can offer practical as well as emotional support. They can share coping techniques that have worked for them. In addition to providing emotional support to each

A support group provides a safe, supportive environment in which to discuss all facets of having herpes and offers both emotional and practical support.

other, people in support groups share useful information, such as new treatments.

Support groups can be in-person groups or online. Your doctor or the local hospital or clinic may be able to provide information on support groups that meet in your area. You can also do an online search for "herpes support group [your city or town]." In addition, many of the organizations listed in the For More Information section of this resource provide information on support groups or local chapters that hold meetings.

In an online support group, people share information over the Internet. Major search engine sites, such as Google and Yahoo! Groups, often include informal support groups for people with diseases, including herpes. Type "herpes support group online" into the search box. When dealing with advice you receive from people over the Internet, remember that it is just like talking to people in person. The information you get is the result of their personal experiences and opinions. Although you might want to test their dating tips, before you follow any health advice, be sure to check with a health professional such as your doctor.

Finally, there are hotlines, such as the National Herpes Hotline ([919] 361-8488 or [800] 227-8922), which can provide you with encouragement and information about symptoms, support groups, and helpful resources.

GLOSSARY

antiviral medication A medication that keeps viruses from replicating.

bacterium (plural: bacteria) A single-celled organism that causes infections.

Caesarian section A process in which a baby is delivered through an incision in the abdomen.

chromosomes The elements in cells made up of DNA, which form the genetic blueprint of an organism.

chronic Going on for a long time.

contagious Capable of being spread from person to person.

corticosteroids Chemicals secreted by the body that prepare it to deal with a threat.

Crohn's disease An ailment in which a person's bowels become inflamed.

deactivate Make inactive.

DNA Deoxyribonucleic acid. The material that encodes genetic information.

dormant Inactive but alive.

false negative A test result that shows you don't have the disease when you do.

false positive A test result that shows you have a disease when you don't.

gene Part of a chromosome that contains the genetic code for one characteristic or component of the body.

genital Related to the external reproductive organs.

gland An organ that produces a chemical that affects the body.

hormone A chemical in the body that controls a body process.

inhibit To keep from performing any activity.

intravenous Put into a vein.

latency A period during which a virus remains inactive but still present in the body.

lupus A disease in which a person's immune system attacks his or her own body.

mucous membranes The tissue that lines areas such as the mouth and secretes mucus.

nucleus The area in the center of a cell that contains the chromosomes.

organism A living creature.

Pap smear A test done periodically on women in which a small sample of vaginal tissue, usually the uterine cervix, is checked for cancer cells.

permeates Soaks into.

perspective Point of view.

poultice A hot mass of bread or meal and herbs placed on the skin.

profile In genetics, an arrangement of DNA from a particular organism.

replicate To make copies of.

stigmatize To label as bad and exclude from activities.

suppress To make less effective.

topical Relating to something put on the skin.

virulent Very harmful.

FOR MORE INFORMATION

Canadian Federation for Sexual Health
2197 Riverside Drive, Suite 403
Ottawa, ON K1H 7X3
Canada
(613) 241-4474
Website: http://www.cfsh.ca
This is an organization composed of
    volunteers that promotes sexual health
    education and provides community health
    services in this area.

Centers for Disease Control (CDC)
National Center for AIDS/HIV, Viral Hepatitis,
    STD, and TB Prevention
1600 Clifton Road
Atlanta, GA 30329
(800) 232-4636
Website: http://www.cdc.gov/nchhstp
This division works to prevent the spread of
    STDs and provides data and information to
    the public.

Partnership for Prevention
1015 18th Street NW, Suite 300
Washington, DC 20036
(202) 833-0009
Website: http://www.prevent.org/Initiatives/
    National-Coalition-for-Sexual-Health.aspx
One of this organization's initiatives is the
    Coalition for Sexual Health, which advocates
    for top-notch health information and
    health services. It also provides news and
    publications.

Planned Parenthood Federation of America
434 West 33rd Street
New York, NY 10001
(212) 541-7800
Website: http://www.plannedparenthood.org
In addition to contraception information,
    Planned Parenthood provides resources for
    dealing with and preventing STDs.

Sex Information and Education Council of
    Canada (SIECCAN)
850 Coxwell Avenue
Toronto, ON M4C 5R1
Canada
(416) 466-5304
Website: http://www.sieccan.org
SIECCAN works to promote sexual health and
    educate the public. It provides a list of
    resources on sexual health.

WEBSITES

Because of the changing nature of Internet links,
Rosen Publishing has developed an online list
of Web sites related to the subject of this book.
This site is updated regularly. Please use this
link to access the list:

http://www.rosenlinks.com/YSH/Herp

FOR FURTHER READING

Ambrose, MaryLou. *Investigating STDs*. Berkeley Heights, NJ: Enslow Publishers, 2010.

Collins, Nicholas, and Samuel J. Wood. *Frequently Asked Questions About STDs (FAQ: Teen Life)*. New York, NY: Rosen Publishing, 2011.

Cozic, Charles. *Herpes*. San Diego, CA: Reference Point Press, 2010.

Espejo, Roman. *Sexually Transmitted Diseases*. Chicago, IL: Greenhaven Press, 2011.

Feinstein, Stephen. *Sexuality and Teens: What You Should Know About Sex, Abstinence, Birth Control, Pregnancy, and STDs*. Berkeley Heights, NJ: Enslow Publishers, 2009.

Ford, Carol, and Elizabeth Shimer Bower. *Living with Sexually Transmitted Diseases*. New York, NY: Facts On File, 2009.

Hasler, Nikol. *Sex: A Book for Teens: An Uncensored Guide to Your Body, Sex, and Safety*. San Francisco, CA: Zest Books, 2010.

Hunter, Miranda, and William Hunter. *Sexually Transmitted Infections*. Broomall, PA: Mason Crest, 2013.

Parks, Peggy J. *Sexually Transmitted Diseases*. San Diego, CA: Reference Point Press, 2014.

Scott, Jess, and Matt Posner. *Teen Guide to Sex and Relationships*. JessInk, 2012.

Watkins, Heidi. *Sexually Transmitted Infections*. Chicago, IL: Greenhaven Press, 2011.

Wolny, Philip. *I Have an STD. Now What?* (Teen Life 411). New York, NY: Rosen Publishing, 2015.

BIBLIOGRAPHY

Andrews, John. *Herpes*. Amazon Digital Services, 2011.

Centers for Disease Control and Prevention. "Genital Herpes—CDC Fact Sheet." February 13, 2013. Retrieved November 2, 2014 (http://www.cdc.gov/std/herpes/stdfact-herpes-detailed.htm).

EssentialLifeSkills.net. "Effective Goal-Setting." Retrieved September 20, 2014 (http://www.essentiallifeskills.net/effectivegoalsetting.html).

Guttmacher Institute. "American Teens' Sexual and Reproductive Health." Retrieved September 28, 2014 (http://www.guttmacher.org/pubs/FB-ATSRH.html).

Herpes-Coldsores Support Network. "Herpes Statistics." Retrieved September 15, 2014 (http://www.herpes-coldsores.com/herpes_statistics.htm).

McFarland, John. "Brief Overview of the Herpes Virus." Retrieved September 15, 2014 (http://www.austincc.edu/microbio/2704y/hsv.htm).

Medline Plus/National Institutes of Health. "Genital Herpes." Retrieved September 16, 2014 (http://www.nlm.nih.gov/medlineplus/ency/article/000857.htm).

Medline Plus/National Institutes of Health. "Sexually Transmitted Diseases." Retrieved September 5, 2014 (http://www.nlm.nih.gov/medlineplus/sexuallytransmitteddiseases.html).

MIT Medical. "Everything You Should Know about Herpes." Retrieved September 28, 2014

(http://medweb.mit.edu/wellness/programs/
herpes.html#alternatives).

New Zealand Herpes Foundation. "Herpes—The
Facts." Retrieved September 6, 2014 (http://
www.herpes.org.nz/patient-info/key-facts/).

Seventeen. "Talking to Your Parents About Sex."
Retrieved September 25, 2014 (http://www.
seventeen.com/health/tips/sex-parents-
hsp-0404).

Skills You Need. "Decision Making—An
Introduction." Retrieved September 20, 2014
(http://www.skillsyouneed.com/ips/decision-
making.html).

Stanford University. "Historical Background."
Retrieved September 15, 2014 (https://virus.
stanford.edu/herpes/History.html).

Teller County Public Health. "101 Ways to Say
No to Sex." Retrieved September 18, 2014
(http://www.co.teller.co.us/
publichealth/101WaysToSayNoToSex.aspx).

University of California, Santa Barbara, Sociology
Department. "Psychological Issues Related
to Herpes." Retrieved September 25, 2014
(http://www.soc.ucsb.edu/sexinfo/article/
psychological-issues-related-herpes).

Web MD Genital Herpes Health Center. "Dating
with Herpes." Retrieved September 26, 2014
(http://www.webmd.com/genital-herpes/
guide/genital-herpes-reentering-dating-scene).

Ybanez, Christine. Herpes Simplex Virus. Lexing-
ton, KY: SMGC Publishing, 2012.

INDEX

ABOUT THE AUTHOR

Jeri Freedman has a B.A. from Harvard University. For fifteen years she worked for companies in the medical field. She is the author of numerous young adult nonfiction books, including *Hemophilia, Lymphoma: Current and Emerging Trends in Detection and Treatment, How Do We Know About Genetics and Heredity?, The Mental and Physical Effects of Obesity, Everything You Need to Know About Genetically Modified Foods, Autism,* and *Hepatitis B.*

PHOTO CREDITS:

Cover, p. 1 Visuals Unlimited, Inc./Veronika Burmeister/Getty Images; cover (inset left) Image Point Fr/Shutterstock.com; cover (inset right) Catherine Yeulet/iStock/Thinkstock; p. 5 Echo/Cultura/Getty Images; pp. 8, 14, 26, 35, 46 mathagraphics/Shutterstock.com; p. 8 (bottom) John Watney/Science Source/Getty Images; pp. 9, 10 SPL/Science Source; pp. 12, 15 Biophoto Associates/Science Source/Getty Images; p. 17 Will & Deni McIntyre/Science Source/Getty Images; p. 20 Biology Media/Science Source/Getty Images; p. 23 Southern Illinois University/Science Source/Getty Images; p. 27 Joe Schilling/The Life Picture Collection/Getty Images; p. 29 Sam Edwards/Caiaimage/Getty Images; p. 33 Ariel Skelley/Blend Images/Getty Images; p. 36 Peter Dazeley/Photographer's Choice/Getty Images; p. 37 CDC/Dr. Craig Lyerla; p. 39 Photo Researchers/Science Source/Getty Images; p. 41 Jose Luis Pelaez Inc/Blend Images/Getty Images; p. 47 Nicole S. Young/E+/Getty Images; p. 48 Ghislain & Marie David de Lossy/The Image Bank/Getty Images; p. 52 Smith Collection/Taxi/Getty Images; p. 53 Zigy Kaluzny/The Image Bank/Getty Images; cover and interior pages (patterns and textures) PinkPueblo/Shutterstock.com, Slanapotam/Shutterstock.com, Samarttiw/Shutterstock.com, elen_studio/Shutterstock.com, Sfio Cracho/Shutterstock.com; interior pages (caduceus) Actor/Shutterstock.com; back cover Sergey Nivens/Shutterstock.com.

Designer: Michael Moy ; Editor: Kathy Kuhtz Campbell